I0147325

Alfred Williams Haywood

Speech of A. W. Haywood, Esq.,

of Counsel for the defense, in the trial of Dr. Eugene Grissom:

Superintendent, North Carolina Insane Asylum, July 17, 1890; being the

third speech delivered for the defense, the speech of Hon. Thomas C.

Fuller

Alfred Williams Haywood

Speech of A. W. Haywood, Esq.,
of Counsel for the defense, in the trial of Dr. Eugene Grissom: Superintendent, North Carolina Insane Asylum, July 17, 1890; being the third speech delivered for the defense, the speech of Hon. Thomas C. Fuller

ISBN/EAN: 9783337370640

Printed in Europe, USA, Canada, Australia, Japan

Cover: Foto ©ninafisch / pixelio.de

More available books at **www.hansebooks.com**

SPEECH

OF

A. W. Haywood, Esq.,

OF COUNSEL FOR THE DEFENCE,

IN THE TRIAL OF

DR. EUGENE GRISSOM,

Superintendent North Carolina Insane Asylum,

JULY 17, 1889,

BEING THE THIRD SPEECH DELIVERED FOR THE DEFENCE,
THE SPEECH OF HON. THOMAS C. FULLER BEING
FIRST AND THAT OF MR. T. P. DEVEREUX
BEING THE SECOND.

———————

RALEIGH, N. C.:
EDWARDS & BROUGHTON, STEAM PRINTERS AND BINDERS.
1889.

SPEECH

A. W. HAYWOOD, Esq.,

IN THE GRISSOM CASE.

Mr. President, and Gentlemen of the Board:

In the order of argument which has been agreed upon by the counsel for the respondent, it now becomes my duty to address you.

In doing so, I shall not attempt to cover this case fully, or go into it at great length, for it has been so fully discussed by the gentlemen on our side who have preceded me—Col. Fuller and Mr. Devereux—that to do so would be the work of supererogation.

The case we are now engaged in trying is a new one in North Carolina; it is a case of the first impression here; no such case has ever been tried in the courts of this State. But while it is a novel case in North Carolina, it is by no means novel or unheard of in the other States of this Union. Such prosecutions as this are common and of frequent occurrence, and the fate of nearly every Superintendent who has held his office for as long a time as Dr. Grissom has (twenty-one years), or even half so long. The Superintendent of an insane asylum is an executive officer, charged with the maintenance of discipline, and as such, it becomes his duty, in a long period of years, to discharge many employees. In doing so, necessarily he makes many bitter enemies, who, thirsting for revenge, "bide their time." Sooner or later, some man, actuated by unholy ambition or a greed for office, will be found to take advantage of this discontent and desire for vengeance, and the result is, the Superintendent is dragged into court to answer charges similar, in all respects, to those on which Dr. Grissom is arraigned before the bar of this court to day. Experience has shown that nearly every Superintendent of an insane asylum must, sooner or later, pass through such an ordeal as this respondent is passing through now.

This trial, gentlemen, is novel in another respect. The section of The Code (section 2249) which authorizes it provides as follows, viz.:

" He shall hold his office for six years from and after his appointment, unless sooner removed by said Board, who may, for infidelity to his trust, gross immorality, or incompetency to discharge the duties of his office, *fully proved and declared*, and the proof thereof recorded in the book of their proceedings, remove him and appoint another in his place."

You will observe from the above that this Board has the authority to deprive Dr. Grissom of his property—his office. That an office is as much property as a house is, or as land is, has been settled by the Supreme Court of North Carolina ever since the decision of that Court in the famous case of *Hoke* v. *Henderson*, 4 Devereux's Law, page 17. This proposition will not be denied by the counsel on the other side.

This section of The Code virtually, and in substance, gives you authority to convict Dr. Grissom of a crime, and in the charges preferred against him he is charged with the commission of two if not more crimes, viz.: adultery—which, by section 1041 of The Code, is made a crime and punishable as such; and embezzlement—which, by section 1016 of The Code, is made a crime and punishable as such. I say these charges are preferred in substance, if not in technical language, against this respondent.

This being so, the rules which obtain in the trial of a criminal case in a criminal court must obtain here; and you must be satisfied, beyond a reasonable doubt, that Dr. Grissom is guilty of these charges, before you can find him guilty. This is the rule in criminal courts, under the laws of the State, and having no rules laid down, in the statute under which we are proceeding, for your guidance, you must follow and be guided by the rules established in criminal courts. At the beginning of this trial, the other side contended that this was an investigation. But when the prosecution had put in their evidence and rested their case, and we began to put in ours, they spoke of it as a trial, as an indictment, &c., and they invoked to their aid all the technicalities known to the criminal lawyer, and all the rules governing trials upon indictments, in excluding what they could of our evidence. That it is a trial, and not an investigation, being now admitted on both sides, then this trial must be conducted, as nearly as possible, in analogy to a trial upon an indictment; and you must be satisfied, beyond a reasonable doubt, of the respondent's guilt, and you must give him the benefit of every doubt, before you can convict him. The law accords this much to the vilest criminal.

Again, gentlemen, this trial is peculiar and unusual in another respect:

Under this section of The Code, Dr. Grissom can be brought up before the bar of this court and made to answer for every act, every deed, and every word, yes, almost for every thought, of his life for the past twenty-one years. Have you thought of this, gentlemen? Has it occurred to you what latitude the statute gives you, when trying the Superintendent? Call the roll of the public officers of North Carolina, and tell me which of them can be subjected to such an ordeal as this respondent is subjected to here to-day. Can you force your Governor, or any of your judges or members of Congress or the Legislature, or any of your public officers or any private citizen, to submit himself to such a test? No. Think of it, I say—compelled here to-day to answer before this tribunal for every deed, every act, every hasty, idle or

angry word, done or spoken during the past twenty-one
years! Gentlemen, how many of us could stand the ordeal?
I ask the prosecutors in this case—I ask the counsel on the
other side—I ask the Board—I ask every one in the sound of
my voice, if they would not shrink from such a trial—such an
ordeal, such a test? No such trial could take place in any other
court in North Carolina. It comes nearer—I say it rever-
ently—that last and awful trial, which we must all undergo
in that final day, when we stand before that tribunal from
which no appeal lies, than anything I can conceive of.

And now, after months—even years—of secret, silent and
tireless preparation, by the prosecutors, for this day and hour
(for this unhallowed conspiracy was not hatched yesterday,
and we only see now, in the light of day, the result of many a
night's dark and secret plotting and planning to ruin this
gray-haired old man), after scouring and raking, as with a
fine-tooth comb, this State, from the mountains to the sea-
shore—from the Virginia line to the South Carolina line—
for some hasty word or act of this respondent, what charges,
and what evidence to sustain them, do they submit to you
here to-day? They offer evidence which they claim tends
to sustain three charges—immorality, cruelty and misappro-
priating; all of which, when subjected to the test of reason
and probability, simmer down to almost nothing, as I will
show you.

First, let's examine the charges and specifications, and
see how many of them are eliminated from your consideration, by reason of no evidence whatever having been offered
in their support.

They are as follows:

Under the charge of immorality—

" *Specification* 4.—That, at some time during the year 1887,
said Superintendent made improper and insulting advances,
at and in said asylum, to Miss Delia F. Morris, an attendant
of said institution."

Not an iota of proof offered to sustain this charge.

"*Specification* 5. That, at some time during the year 1887, the said Superintendent, at and in said asylum, made improper and insulting advances to Miss Rosa Bryan, an attendant of said institution."

Not a particle of evidence to sustain this charge.

Under the charge of cruelty—

"*Specification* 5. That, at some time during the year 1887, it was made known to said Superintendent that one of the attendants had personally assaulted Mrs. Summerlin, a patient under his charge, for disobeying an order of said attendant, yet the said Superintendent kept in his service the said attendant."

Not one word of evidence to sustain this charge.

"*Specification* 6. That, at some time during the winter of 1887, said Superintendent choked W. C. Pridgen, a blind patient under his charge, the same not being done in self-defence."

No evidence offered to sustain this charge.

"*Specification* 13. That, at some time during 1887, the said Superintendent ordered an attendant to duck the Rev. Elisha R. Britton, a patient under his charge, in a bath-tub, without any just reason for so doing."

This charge was abandoned in open court.

Neither has a scintilla of evidence been offered, or any pretence been made, to support the charges as to Miss Davis, Mrs. Oglesby and Mrs. Perdue.

So that eight of them are eliminated from your consideration, and, as to them, you will find a verdict of not guilty.

The cases upon which any evidence of any nature whatever has been offered, are as follows, then, viz.: Miss Burch, Mrs. Perkinson, Miss Edwards, Mrs. Floyd, Mrs. Overman, Mrs. Whaley, Mrs. Howle, W. P. Upchurch, Mike Cosgrove, Henry Cone, J. D. L. Smith, Perry Boyd, Kennedy and Williams, J. C. Hervey, Robert Barnett, Jonathan Bass, John Nutt, Zeb. Williams, Mr. Wortham, Mrs. Lowther and Mrs. Gaskin.

Of this number, Miss Ella N. Edwards, the witness who seriously swears to you that the first order she received from Dr. Grissom, when she first came here, was to treat the patients like " wild cats"—Miss Edwards, the swift witness— the young woman who corresponds with Dr. Rogers, and calls him "sweetheart," and whom he visits, under an assumed name, at a dress-maker's house in this city—the young woman with whose person he is seen to take liberties—the modest, retiring, bashful, blushing young woman of eighteen, who walks through half a dozen lawyers to shake her fist in Dr. Grissom's face—is the sole and only witness, as to six of them. This fact alone eliminates these six cases from your consideration, for she is wholly unworthy of belief, and no credit can attach to her testimony, as I will show you further on. Besides, see how wild and improbable is the tale she swore to here! She swore that Dr. Grissom, as an act of cruelty, put pegs in the mouth of Miss Lutie Roberts. Both Dr. Grissom and Mr. Guthrie explain to you that this was merely a method of forced alimentation. She swore that Mrs. Howle told her that Dr. Grissom had kissed her, and at the same time stated that Mrs. Howle had no mind whatever. Mrs. Howle's husband comes on the stand, as a witness in behalf of Dr. Grissom, and gives the lie to this testimony. That he put Mrs. Whaley and Mrs. Overman in a room and told them to fight, whereas Dr. Grissom explains and tells you that they never fought, and would not have been permitted to fight; that they were only in the room together for a minute, while he and an attendant stood at the door, and that he merely made the statement to them, in the presence of each other and of the attendant, in order to frighten them, and show them the impropriety of their conduct. That he threw water in the face of Miss Mary Foy. Dr. Grissom admits that, on one occasion, he threw water in the face of Miss Foy for the purpose of making a mental impression on her; and it is not denied that it is a proper mode of treatment. And as to Miss Nancy Flood, the idea that Dr. Grissom would knock down and choke and curse a woman is so preposterous as to merit only a smile of incredulity.

Of another case—Perry Boyd—the only witness is T. J. Harris, whom we have proven to have the reputation of a common liar and a seducer of women—a man who was charged with stealing a patient's coat, and selling it to a negro; a man who signed a "lie bill," acknowledging he had slandered Miss Nora Burch; and a man who did not deny, on the stand here, having debauched a female attendant while he was an employee of this institution.

And now, taking up the charges upon which any respectable evidence is offered, in the order in which they appear in the charges filed, we first come to the charge of sexual intercourse with Miss Nora Burch.

You will remember, gentlemen, the evidence as to this charge and specification is about as follows:

Mr. W. R. King testifies that on one Saturday afternoon, last of July or first of August, he was standing at the corner of the stage, and he saw Miss Burch enter the patients' parlor, and that she shut the door, leaving a crack in the door about as wide as his (King's) two fingers; that soon afterwards he saw Dr. Grissom enter the room and lock the door; that he knew he locked the door, because he heard the key turn; that soon after Dr. Grissom entered the room he (King)—having remained on the stage four or five minutes—sneaked and crawled up to the door and looked through the key-hole; that he saw Dr. Grissom and Miss Burch in the act of sexual intercourse; that Miss Burch's limbs were exposed; that the foot of the bed was towards the door, and the head of it in an opposite direction; that the foot of the bed was just far enough removed from the door to permit of its being opened; that they were lying lengthwise the bed. And he further states that at that time there was no one else on the floor except himself, Dr. Grissom and Miss Burch, and that he was up there for the purpose of fixing the scenery; that he had been sent there by Mrs. Lawrence, and that it was not his custom to come on that floor unless ordered to do so. He further testifies that Mrs. Lawrence never gave him an order, or sent him, to fix the scenery but once; and in this respect Mrs. Lawrence confirms his statement.

The next witness, Emanuel Jones, testifies that he was up here on one Saturday evening, and that he went from the chapel, where he had concealed himself, to Mrs. Lawrence's bed-room door, and he, too, looked through the key-hole; and he describes the location of the bed as King did Both of them testified that they saw Dr. Grissom have sexual intercourse with Miss Burch; that they saw the soles of their feet; that they were lying with their feet towards the door. He says further that King met him afterwards, and asked him what he was doing looking through that key-hole that Saturday afternoon, and when he told him what he was doing, King made no reply—only laughed. Now, I want to call your attention to that. King says there was nobody on the floor but himself, Dr. Grissom and Miss Burch. Jones swears he was there also; that King saw him looking through the key-hole. Afterwards King reads the newspapers. He sees the conflict between the testimony of Jones and that of his own. He is recalled, and comes back on the stand a week afterwards, and tries to make his testimony fit in with Jones' by taking back his statement that he was the only one on the floor, besides Dr. Grissom and Miss Burch, on that Saturday afternoon in July or August This attempt to patch his testimony is suspicious. This man King, who sneaks and crawls—(W)hole-Peeping King—comes back and tries to make his testimony conform to the testimony of Jones. Why, gentlemen, do you not know that he did not see Jones on that occasion? He saw the conflict of testimony; he saw it would be fatal, and he tries to correct it by saying that he did ask Jones about what he was doing there that Saturday afternoon. But he did not go quite far enough—he forgot something; for when he was first on the stand he furthermore said that the only persons he told, or talked to, about this matter, were, first, Mr. Ball, Mr. Thompson next, and then Dr. Rogers. He forgot to mention Jones; but now he comes back and swears he told it also to Emanuel Jones. Now, as to Jones, I think it hardly worth while to discuss him. He is a proven liar. Any witness who will get up here and tell you, on his oath, that he happened to be down town, and a strange man met him, whom he did not know, and whom he had never seen before, and asked him to go to a certain office, and that he followed him in the dark and found himself in Mr. Whitaker's office—don't you know he is lying? You know as well as I do that he knew what he was going up in that office for. When you get to the cross-examination of Jones you will see that it is full of contradictions— that from beginning to end he is lying. Besides, he says on the stand: "My feelings towards Dr. Grissom are feelings of enmity."

The other witness who testified to this matter is Mr. West, and his testimony amounts to nothing. He merely tells you that on two occasions he saw Dr. Grissom and Miss Burch enter the sitting-room; this amounts to nothing, for Dr. Grissom and other witnesses explain it. What is the evidence on the other side? Dr. Grissom tells you that on several occasions he met Miss Burch in the Matron's room, where she went to report to him as Superintendent, and also that vaginal examinations of Miss Burch were made by him in the Matron's bed-room, with the knowledge of the Matron, and at which she, the Matron, was sometimes present. Dr. Grissom tells you that he was treating Miss Burch for troubles peculiar to women. He tells you that she was chief attendant, and that it was her duty to make reports to him, and that he frequently met her in this room for the purpose of getting her reports; that he was treating her for these troubles with the knowledge of Mrs. Lawrence, and with her approval, and Mrs. Lawrence verifies that statement, and says that frequently she was present. Mrs. Burch, Miss

Nora's mother, testifies to the same effect; her sister also
gives her testimony to the same effect.

Now, take all these witnesses; put their testimony against
that of Peeping King and this lying negro boy, and are you
not satisfied that King and Jones were bound to be lying
when they testified as to what they saw that Saturday afternoon? They say they saw Dr. Grissom have sexual intercourse with Miss Nora Burch. King said he saw the door
left open as wide as his two fingers when Miss Burch went
in. Now, it is physically impossible for any one to stand
upon that stage and tell whether that door is open or shut;
it cannot be done. He says he heard the key turn in the
lock. Now, that is another physical impossibility—he could
not have heard it to save his life. By slamming the door
you can hear it, but not by shutting the door, as ordinarily
would be done. Shut in the usual way, you could not
hear it at all; and as to hearing the key turn in the lock, it
is an actual impossibility. You have proved this to be true
by your own examination and test.

Again, Mrs. Lawrence tells you that the bed never occupied the position which Jones and King said it occupied.
It never was placed in that room with its foot towards the
door and its head in the position indicated by King and
Jones, and in this she is sustained by the testimony of Miss
McKoy. It was placed with its head towards the partition
wall which separates the bed-room from the parlor. Sometimes, when the door was left open, the head was placed
against the door, but this was at night, and in the summer-
time; but in the day-time the bed did not occupy this last-
named position.

She, Mrs. Lawrence, furthermore tells you, that when she
left that room she darkened it to keep the flies out; that she
rarely ever left home on Saturday afternoons. Dr. Grissom
tells you that this floor was full of attendants and servants
on Saturday afternoons Both Jones and King fixed this
occurrence on Saturday afternoon, in the month of July or

August. At that time, it is testified to that it is the habit to have the floors full of servants, going to and fro, to get clothing, cleaning up, etc. Again—and her testimony settles this charge—Miss McKoy, the young lady whose testimony must have most favorably impressed you, says that she knows the statement of Mrs. Lawrence, in regard to being present on the stage with King, to be true; that at the time Mrs. Lawrence gave that man King directions to fix the scenery, they immediately went on the stage together for that purpose; and that she (Mrs Lawrence) came up on the stage with him, and she was there all the time with him, while he was fixing it. She directed this man King all the time he was on the stage; and that it was in October, and not in July or August. Now, that young lady also said that she was at the head of the sewing department; she saw the stage from the sewing-room, and she saw Mrs. Lawrence with King, and this was in October. She knows it was in October, for she did not come here until October. Mrs. Lawrence says she never gave King but one order to fix the scenery; it was fixed then and at that time; and that she came up on the stage with King immediately on giving the order, and remained there with him until it was fixed. King says she never gave him but one order to fix the scenery. I think if Miss McKoy's testimony had been published in the papers before Mr. King was recalled to the stand, he would have changed his testimony more than he did; for I want you to bear it in mind, that Mrs. Lawrence is sustained in every particular by Miss Koy, both as to the location of that bed and as to being on the stage with King. Miss McKoy stands before you an unimpeached and unimpeachable witness. So we have Peeping King and a lying negro on one side—Dr. Grissom, Mrs. Lawrence and Miss McKoy on the other. Mr. Ashley said that by turning on full light in the patients' parlor and opening the door to the hall, he could see the shadows, the hall being darker than the parlor, and thereby could tell whether the door was open or not. But King said nothing about shadows. King said he saw the door left open and then shut. He does not tell you that he knew the door was open by reason of shadows—does not claim that—but says he saw it open as wide as his two fingers. Now, he never saw that door open, nor did he hear the key turn in the lock; that is a physical impossibility. He furthermore tells you that this bed was standing with its foot to the door. The other witnesses tell you that this bed remained in the position Mrs. Lawrence describes. Mrs. Lawrence says the bed was the one she slept on; had a feather bed on it, and had it been disturbed she would have known it; and that it was not disturbed or mashed down. Can it be. that with such evidence on one side, and the character of the evidence we offer on the other, you can find a verdict of guilty on a charge that is intended to disgrace and ruin this man, and cast a stigma on his wife and sons and daughters? Can it be possible that you can be instrumental in the disgrace of a man so eminent, exalted and distinguished in his profession upon such testimony as the prosecution offers you on this charge? Again, this man King, who is the main witness—what has he done? Before he came on this stand he signed a statement in writing. I want to call you gentlemen's attention to that book containing this statement. Mr. Whitaker asked Mr. King this question: " Was all that on the first page written in that book when you signed it ? " He replied : "Some of it " "I have been here three and a half years; was there, I think, but I do not remember anything about immorality." Now, I am going to ask you to examine this book, and see if it does not bear intrinsic evidence that this man signed this book just as it now is. It is evident, from the book itself—not an erasure or interlineation—that he did. This man, who acknowledges that he goes around crawling and sneaking and looking through key-holes, went to Dr. Grissom's office about noon, on Friday preceding this trial, and left without one word of dispute between Dr. Grissom and himself, parted in the best of feeling, and he then made this statement, contained in this book, to Dr. Grissom. He left the room—not one word of an unpleasant nature had occurred; he goes back there again on Friday night and voluntarily makes the same statement. He tells you that Robert Grissom was reducing his statement to writing as he made it. As soon as it was written the book was read to him; then it was handed to him; he turned the pages over slowly, one by one, calmly, and then he signed the statement. Now, remember, this was all before any fuss had occurred between Dr. Grissom and himself; for when he went out of that room he went (as far as we can tell) in perfect friendship. King writes a good hand; he can read writing After reading, page by page, he signed it; and he states in there that he had never seen " *any immorality on the part of Dr. Grissom.*" He leaves the office; during that night some unknown influences seem to be brought to bear upon him, some change comes over him; and the next morning he goes to see Dr. Grissom, and, in an angry tone and bullying manner, says: "I want you to take that part off about Kaylor." Note, gentlemen, he does not even then ask to retract the immorality part. Dr. Grissom says: "Why do you ask it?" and King replies: "Because Kaylor has never done me any harm, and besides, I do not want you to ever talk to me any more about this thing." His manner was so insulting, that Dr. Grissom says: "Do you come here to bully me? If you do, I will kill you." And King replied: "Shoot on; I am as good a man as you are." Now, this does not take place until the morning after King had made his statement in writing and signed it. It is no use to claim that this witness was intimidated by Dr. Grissom into signing this paper, for no difficulty had occurred between them up to the time of signing the book, and he is not a man who can be intimidated. On the stand here he was very defiant and acted the bully, as you saw.

Among all the charges brought against Dr. Grissom, the most serious one is this of sexual intercourse with Miss Nora

Burch, a lady who proved a most excellent character here by all her neighbors, but who is, unfortunately, now insane. Had not that poor girl, Nora Burch, been stricken by God and her lips sealed by silence, she would be here to-day to answer these slanders of King and Jones. It is passing strange that it is an insane woman who has been selected as the object of slander, out of all the female attendants who have been here. Her lips are sealed by the curse of God, as if with the seal of death; that is why she cannot be here at this time. I would that she were here to answer to the vile, dirty and slanderous testimony of Plummer King and Emanuel Jones. I want you to note that King and Jones have selected her for their calumny and malice. They feel that they can slander her with impunity; she has lost her reason and cannot deny. Would to God she could!

And now I will proceed to the next charge—

"That at some time during the spring of 1887, said Superintendent, at and in said asylum and elsewhere, made immoral and lecherous proposals and advances to Mrs. Lillie B. Perkinson, the wife of an employee of said institution."

Now, gentlemen, it seems to me that the evidence of this lady is of such a character as to convince you that she is not telling the truth. She tells you that on four or five separate occasions, covering a long period of time, Dr. Grissom made indecent proposals to her, and that she immediately reported them to her husband. She tells you further that her husband continued to be in the employment of Dr. Grissom for over a year afterwards; that *she* continued to solicit employment for him, *and time and time again to ask favors for him of Dr. Grissom;* that after her husband left the asylum, she came and begged Dr. Grissom to get him a place with Dr. Skinner. Now, gentlemen, do you not know that these things could never have taken place, and that if they had, her husband would not have remained in Dr. Grissom's employment? You know there is no man who would submit to anything of the sort. You know if this lady had told her husband of these indignities which she said Dr. Grissom had offered her, he would have left his employment, and if he had one drop of Anglo-Saxon blood in his veins he would have called Dr. Grissom to an account; but not one word did he say upon that subject; no complaint was ever made by him to anybody of Dr. Grissom's conduct. Why did they not put him on the stand and let him verify his wife's statement? Why did he not come and say, "As soon as I heard it I became angry, and went to Dr. Grissom and told him I would hold him to account"? Why, gentlemen, it is beyond belief, that this lady could have been telling the truth. I do not believe that man lives in North Carolina who would submit to being told by his wife of such things as these, and then go and seek employment from the man who had wronged him—and seek it time and time again. It is not true; it is not reasonable. Besides, she told you here on the stand that she was actuated by revenge and that she thought her day for getting even had come. Again, we had evidence attacking her character, but you would not admit it.

If there is any evidence more incredible than that of Mrs. Perkinson, it is that of Miss Edwards. There is something very peculiar about Miss Edwards' testimony. In the first place, she knows more than any other witness who has testified in this case. Miss Edwards knew everything that was going on in the institution, whether in her ward or in any other ward, and all about it If you will take Dr. Rogers' letter to "Dear May," and compare it with Miss Edwards' testimony, you will see that she is familiar with the contents of that letter all the way through. It is almost certain that she had received a letter similar to the one "Dear May" received. If you, gentlemen, will take that letter and Miss Edwards' testimony and compare them, you · will see that she has "plumbed the line," and, after going on and reading that letter carefully, you will find that she has sworn to the same things that Dr. Rogers' letter to

H—2

"Dear May" suggested she should swear to. Again, her conduct on the stand was such as not to leave the impression that she was "modest and retiring." She flaunted herself into the room, on a hot July day, adorned with jewelry, a silk cloak and a silk dress, and then rushed through Dr. Grissom's half-dozen lawyers, and shook her fist in his face. She tells you, on her oath, that she is actuated by revenge, as does Mrs. Perkinson ; they both tell you it is for the purpose of " getting even with Dr. Grissom " that they are here. If I ever saw a female witness on the stand, in any court, who was bold and brazen, and whose conduct betokened less of a lady, it was Miss Edwards. Never in my life before—never in my experience as a lawyer—have I seen a female witness walk through a group of half-dozen lawyers to shake her fist in the face of the respondent. I am not accustomed to this type of a modest, virtuous girl. I do not suppose it ever occurred before in any court in this State, yet she is supposed to be a modest, innocent girl, who has been wronged and injured by the advances of this respondent. Do you believe it?

Again, did you notice, when Col. Fuller, in his cross-examination of Miss Edwards, asked her how she directed her letters to Dr. Rogers, how she showed signs of guilty terror? Now, you will remember that in the " Dear May " letter she is instructed *how to begin* and *how to end :* what *to say*, and *how to send the letters, to whose care*, etc. Dr. Rogers gives her minute directions about the whole matter, and puts words in her mouth to say. When Col. Fuller asked Ella N. Edwards how she began her letters to Dr. Rogers, and how she signed them, she turned as white as a sheet, hesitated, and seemed not to know what to say. I know she thought that Col. Fuller knew about that letter of instruction, which we feel certain Dr. Rogers sent her. She hesitated, she twisted and she turned, and finally said: "Dr. Rogers." Col. Fuller said : "I do not mean on the outside of the let-

ter." Then she hesitated and stammered, and turned white
and then red, and answered: "That is none of your business." In a matter of this sort, all these little things tell;
they are the links that make the chain.

You were told at the beginning of this trial that we expected to show that this testimony was manufactured and
obtained by unlawful means. We are now taking up all
these little facts and putting them together; and it goes to
show what we have told you was true; it goes to show a conspiracy—manufactured testimony—and that Miss Edwards
had received a letter similar to the "Dear May" letter, and
it was that letter which made her come here and testify.
Now, another reason why her evidence can be given no credence is this: She confesses to you, herself, that Dr. Rogers
visited her, under an assumed name, at the house of a dressmaker in this city; and it has been proven by witnesses that
she was seen with Dr. Rogers' arm around her; that she
tried to "palm him off" for a Mr. Edwards, her cousin. She
registered here at a hotel on this occasion, when she came
here as a witness, and gave a false place of residence. Her
whole conduct has been that of concealment, secrecy and
fraud. It is in evidence also that on one occasion a telegram
was received for her at a late hour of the night—about midnight; that Dr. Grissom directed the telegram to be sent to
her by the night attendant. Instead of that being done,
Dr. Rogers took that telegram, himself, to her in her bedroom, in the dead hour of the night. She tells you that,
instead of having Dr. Fuller or Dr. Grissom to attend her,
she selected Dr. Rogers, an unmarried man, as her physician, and a visitor in her room. All this is her own testimony. Taking it all together, it must be very obvious to
you, gentlemen, that her testimony is not to be relied on,
and is not worthy of credit in any prosecution to which her
friend Dr. Rogers is a party.

Again, she says she told Dr. Grissom, when she left here
on a visit to see her sick mother, that she never intended to

return; but the Rev. Mr. Whitaker, on his examination, testifies to you that he had a conversation with her on the train when she was on her way to her mother's house, and she told him she had no fault to find with the Asylum; that Dr. Grissom was so kind, and, in short, everything he ought to be; that she was going to return, whether her mother lived or died, &c. Now, gentlemen, what reliance can be put in such testimony as this of Miss Edwards?

Now as to—

Charge 2—" That Dr. Eugene Grissom, while Superintendent of said asylum, has been guilty of mismanagement of, and cruelty to, patients under his charge, and of perpetrating indignities upon them."

I wish, under this head, to submit for your consideration a few remarks, and to read you some authorities on the subject.

From the character of the evidence introduced by the prosecution, and from the parade which has been made over the bed-strap, which has been produced before you, it would seem that counsel on the other side are trying to make it appear to you that strapping is, *in itself*, cruel; that it is a cruel and unusual mode of treatment, and the mere fact that this apparatus (bed-strap), which has been shown you, was and is used in this institution, is evidence of cruelty on the part of Dr. Grissom. Now, if I can satisfy you that such is not the case, then most of the prosecutors' case falls to the ground. Instead of these methods of treatment being cruel, they are humane and for the best interests of the insane, and are in use in most of the leading asylums of the country. Dr. Grissom has, for many years, openly and publicly, with voice and pen, advocated " Mechanical Protection " for the violent insane, and at the meeting of the " Association of Superintendents of American Institutions for the Insane," held at St. Louis, Mo., he read an article on the subject, which was received by the said association with great approval and endorsed by it. I will read you some portions of this article:

"The insane man, with feelings or inclination, disordered by diseases, with excess of irritability, with loss of will-power adequately to control his appetite, tossed hither and thither by his emotions and passions (the offspring of a diseased brain), sometimes without memory, always without intelligent judgment, perhaps rent and torn by epileptic shocks or driven to suicide or homicide, needs, above all things, protection from himself. He needs, at the hands of his fellow-man, rest and comfort, aid and protection against his changed self. A proposition so self-evident need not detain us. It is undisputed. Such a thing as absolute non-restraint of the insane is utterly unknown, except, perhaps, among the Malays, where mutual slaughter finally effects restraint.

"With equal propriety, when Dr. Sayre wraps a victim of Pott's disease in a plaster jacket, or fits a leg in complicated but ingenious apparatus, to prevent injury by motion or while in sleep, to cure deformity, may be accused of cruel and inhuman restraint. The patient, under a capital surgical operation, is held, to prevent him from injuring himself amid uncontrollable pain, and sometimes he is bound to the operating table. Yet, does not the very hand of humanity hold him most securely? Necessary restraint is as truly a blessing to him, who would otherwise dash out his brains, as the crutch is to the shrunken limb or the cane to the wearied frame. If, as we have seen, the sane must necessarily control, or, if you please, restrain the insane, as the very erection of hospitals provides for, the true question for the medical mind is, how shall it be best accomplished when required? We have to choose between the hypnotic power of drugs, affording the 'chemical restraint of the brain cell,' or the manual restraint of the strong arms of attendants, or that of solitary imprisonment in seclusion, as advocated and employed by our English brethren, or the mechanical restraint of a strap, restraining the patient to a chair, a camisole or a muff or the covered bed. There are patients who maltreat others; who will cut or bruise or otherwise injure themselves; who would tear off their clothing; who would wear themselves to death by maniacal exhaustion, with ceaseless muscular struggles; who would devour abominations; outrage the decencies and sensibilities remaining to their fellow-patients; make day and night a perpetual torment to themselves and all within their reach; retarding their own and the cure of others and hopelessly prolonging their sufferings. Which of the above means of restraint shall we employ?

"Mechanical restraint is far better, we believe, in many cases:

"1. Because of the absence of the personal antagonism between the attendant and the patient, sure to arouse evil passions, stirring to excitement, and followed by proportionate depression.

"2. Because of the certainty and uniformity of its action, unaffected by momentary strength or weakness, by sudden access of feeling or the impatient weariness of fatigue.

"3. Because it does not excite the passions of the patient by the mere sight of disturbance in the overwrought and worn-out attendant.

"4. Because, when recognized as irresistible, it may be said to establish an environment, which the patient accepts, as there is no hope of suddenly overcoming it.

"6. Because it is better than the physical exhaustion of the patient, from contests with attendants, which may be long-continued and serious, even fatal, not infrequently, when the irritability of the patient is great, while his vitality is really low.

"7. Because it may be applied uniformly at night, when necessary, to the suicidal, who could not otherwise be safely cared for, unless at enormous expense, and with the disadvantage of the attendants keeping the patient awake by their presence.

" 8. Because, in a mild form, it may be applied to the homicidal during the day, and still allow him out-door air and exercise with safety.

" 9. Because it may save the cases of violent, acute mania, of whose prognosis we are most hopeful, if no traumatic trouble happens to break down the general vigor of the system. Really, when one considers the history of the provision for the insane, during the past hundred years, both in Europe and in our own country, and reflects that our opponents' claim is only this, that they, from being the representatives of every form of mechanical restraint, have only substituted that of human hands and retained seclusion, there would seem but little to discuss. One feels like saying, with Isaac of old, ' the voice is the voice of Jacob, but the hands are the hands of Esau.'

" 10. Because it is far better for female patients, especially the epileptic and hysterical, than the sight of long-continued struggles with attendants. On the other hand, if manual restraint is only used out of sight, then seclusion is added with its evils."

Again, witness the following from the thirty-seventh report of the Royal Asylum at Perth for 1864:

" Notwithstanding every care taken to prevent their occurrence, many unforeseen assaults have been committed during the year—not unfrequently on the attendants placed in special charge of dangerous patients. We may add, by the way, that such accidents would scarcely have occurred under the old regime of manual restraint, which, with all its faults, had its advantages, and which undoubtedly saved, in more than one form, many lives that are now sacrificed to the popular creed. ' non-restraint,' absurdly so-called. The fact cannot be doubted that reaction against the errors and absurdities of the ' absolute non-restraint' system is setting in

strongly. Asylum physicians find that mechanical restraint
is the most humane mode of treating certain exceptional
phases of insanity—the only mode, apparently, of avoiding
certain catastrophes now of common occurrence; and they
are gradually readopting the mildest forms thereof compati-
ble with the safety or security of their patients. But with
the present strong public feelings in favor of unqualified
non-restraint—the total abolition or absence of restraint in
or under all its forms or names—a feeling which is not
founded on experience, but is merely the fruit of the pseudo-
philantropic tendencies of the age—it is exceptional to find
men with the moral courage necessary to the confession that
their experience, if not belief, is antagonistic to the favored
creed or delusion of the time."

And now listen at this, from the forty-fourth report of the
Belfast Hospital for the Insane, Dr. Robert Stewart, Governor
(appointed by the Lord Lieutenant of Ireland):

"Here it may be appropriately stated that, during the
past year the resident physician escaped, almost by a mir-
acle, a sudden and violent termination of his life, having been
attacked on two separate occasions by two male homicidal in-
mates—in the first instance by an attempt at strangulation,
and in the second by a severe stab in the face, close to the eye,
with a sharpened knitting-needle, which, had it entered it,
would most likely have been fatal. On two occasions afterwards, the same patients who stabbed the resident physician,
similarly injured two of the male attendants—one on the
face also, the eye having been wounded.

"It is only a few months since one of the Commissioners
of Lunacy in England met with an untimely death. He
was officially visiting a hospital, and passing through a
ward (where it was evident that the risk was taken in order
to display non-seclusion and non-restraint), when, by the
side of the medical superintendent, he was struck in the

temple with a sharpened piece of iron by one of the chronic patients, and died a day or two after."

Again, from the twenty-first annual report of the Worcester (England) Asylum:

"During the past year a suicidal wave has been perceptible in the persons under our care. Several, during the day, made determined efforts upon their lives while in the presence of their guardians. These were all detected, and resulted, fortunately, in no permanent injury. Two, however, of this class, were unfortunately allowed by their attendants to separate themselves from the ever-present supervision essential to their safety, and, in consequence, were enabled to effect their purpose."

Dr. Grissom then goes on to say:

"It may not be improper, however, to give some instances from the case books of the North Carolina Asylum for the Insane, of which I have charge, which will illustrate our clinical practice in regard to the several modes of protective restraint:

"'I. H. *Epilectic Mania.*—Has paroxysms of violent excitement, during which he imagines that himself and others are engaged in building, or tearing down log houses, or other work requiring great force. He is proud of his strength, and, to use his expression, "likes to fout for the fun of the thing." He is restrained to prevent violence to himself and others.

"' D. B. *Chronic Mania.*—Was an open masturbator. At times, excited and noisy at night, and practiced the habit in disgusting excess when he has the free use of his hands. It was directed that they be restrained. In the opinion of the writer, restraint has been of much service in his treatment.

"' V. V. *Chronic Mania.*—A distrustful, suspicious man, who will quietly fix his eyes on some particular person, and, without notice of his intention, seize his victim by the throat in the most determined manner.

"'W. P. R. *Chronic Mania.*—Has paroxysms, during which he will swallow anything practicable. On one occasion swallowed a piece of tin one inch square.

"'W. G. A. *Melancholia.*—Refuses any request whatever. With much persuasion and some force he eats enough to sustain life. Will not permit an action of the bowels if he can prevent it. To prevent urination he places a ligature around the penis. To correct this he is restrained at night and watched in the day.

"'W. H. H. *Melancholia.*—Strong suicidal tendencies. Has attempted to kill himself on several occasions. From his deportment and the character of his delusions, he would probably succeed, if not prevented by restraint at night and being watched during the day.

"'W. G. *Chronic Mania.*—An open, unblushing masturbator; violent to self and others. Consider restraint of hands and out-door freedom better treatment than seclusion.

"'C. L. *Mania.*—Subject to paroxysms of excitement, during which she will use any movable thing as a weapon on selected victims, which she has secreted while in a state of quiet.'"

Again, from an English superintendent of insane asylums:

"But I am sadly perplexed when there comes, through precisely the same channels, the hope-inspiring and the blood-stained streams, almost mingling together the following facts:

"1. That within a few months an attendant was killed by a lunatic in Leicester Asylum.

"2. That one lunatic killed another in Durham County Asylum.

"3. That a lunatic was killed in Greenock Poor-House Asylum, and that an attendant was accused of killing him; and—

"4. That a lunatic was reported to have had his ribs fractured, etc., by an attendant in Northwoods Asylum, both being intoxicated at the time, the assailant being subsequently tried and sentenced in the penalty of a fine of £5 and two months' imprisonment.

"Now, my object is not to attribute the slightest degree of culpability, malpractice or misadventure to any one connected with the above deplorable accidents, but simply to show that there must have been struggle, violence, fury, ferocity previous to the death-blow. Nor in adverting to one hundred and sixty instances of accidents, including several suicides, stated to have occurred within the safe and sacred precincts of asylums in Scotland, in 1874–1875, in the annual report of the Commissioners, which is the only record of such important data that we know of, would we breathe or harbor the suspicion that there was either negligence or carelessness or inadventure, or the absence of such precaution as might have prevented fractures and blows and burns, as our only wish is to direct attention to the sad evidence afforded that 'the millennium has not yet arrived in Bedlam.'"

Nowhere, however, do we find more happy expression on this point than in the report of Dr. Curwin for 1876:

" Experience and knowledge of the habits and feelings of those with whom they are daily brought into contact have led the physicians of the hospitals for the insane in this country to prefer the use of such forms of mechanical restraint to the manual force of four or six persons; for in this latter case there is always sure to be a struggle, and neither the patience of Job, nor the meekness of Moses, nor the love of John are inherent qualities in those who must perform such offices, nor it must be frankly stated, if a judgment can be formed from the tone of their writings, in those who so urgently demand the abolition of all mechanical restraint.

"It is not reasonable to believe—and as a proof of the statement, let any one try it in his own person—that an excited, restless person, suffering from acute maniacal excitement, will be as likely to sleep calmly and refreshingly with one

person holding each arm, and one holding each leg, and a
fifth holding the head, when the disposition, so common when
that number of persons are together, to express freely their
opinion on various subjects, as when the same patient is laid
on the bed and so fastened as to be able to turn from side to
side, but not to rise from the horizontal position, a sleeping
potion administered and everything removed which can
attract attention or cause noise and confusion. Besides, any
one who has witnessed the trial of the two methods must
admit that the latter is infinitely preferable on every account,
not only as far less likely to cause bruises, sprains or injuries
to the patient, but also as much less irritating to the feelings
and passions, and the cause of fewer angry words."

Again:

" It will be remembered by those who were present at the
Nashville meeting in 1874, that Vice-President Walker, then
presiding, at the close of the discussion on this topic, made
the following important declaration from his own personal
experience:

"' I was gratified when visiting the institutions in England—the few I did visit—to find that almost universally,
certainly in four-fifths of the cases, the superintendents
expressed themselves in favor of mechanical restraint, and,
singularly enough, the superintendents lay the blame of non-
restraint upon the Commissioners in Lunacy, and the Commissioners in Lunacy throw it back upon the superintendents. They say the superintendents are emulous, one of
another, to report the smallest number of restraints during
the year. Certainly, in my presence, and that of an American medical friend accompanying me, almost without exception, they expressed their preference for mechanical restraint,
and hoped they would have it established there. From an
experience of over twenty years, and from careful, and I
hope by no means superficial study of this question, I firmly
believe that in the future the practice of our best American
asylums now will become the governing rules of Christen-
dom.' "

When Dr. Grissom had finished reading his article to the Association of Superintendents at St. Louis assembled, several of them submitted remarks of approval and approbation upon it, a few of which I now propose to read you:

By Dr. WALKER: "In regard to the paper of Dr. Grissom, I am free to say I approve of it. It was distinctly moderate, and written in the most conclusive form."

Remarks by Dr. CURWEN: "I do not know that I have anything special to say. I have said all I desired to say in my last annual report, and I do not know that I can add to that or express it better than I did.

"There seems to be a misconception on one point. These cases requiring restraint are like an epidemic; they come periodically; month after month may roll around, and few, if any cases, will be found requiring any restraint whatever, and then there will be a period when quite a number will need to be restrained, to prevent injury to themselves or others, or extreme destruction of clothing or furniture. That has been my experience, and I suppose others have had similar experience. In the discussions on this subject, this fact seems to have been entirely overlooked."

Dr. BLACK, of Virginia, said: "I heartily agree with the sentiment expressed in the paper read by Dr. Grissom and the remarks made by Dr. Gray. I should regard the use of restraint in the same light that I would that of medicine or anything else that would secure control and save my patients from danger. I have adopted this plan, and expect to continue it until I find some good reasons for changing it."

Dr. KENAN, from Georgia, said: "It is useless to occupy the time of this Association, but I must say, in relation to mechanical restraint, that we use it whenever we deem it necessary. I do not think we have enough of it in our institution, or that it has arrived at that perfection which I hope to see. I am but a novice in the treatment of insanity, but think I can convince any gentleman here, without much oratory, that it would not do for us to do away with restraint."

Dr STRONG, of Ohio: "This subject of restraint has been so thoroughly and exhaustively discussed, that I can add nothing. In fact, as presented here, I feel there is but one side to the question. I most cordially and emphatically endorse the views of Dr. Grissom on that subject."

Dr. BOUGHTON, of Wisconsin: "I am quite sure there is no division of opinion among us in regard to mechanical protection."

Dr. BARTLETT, Minnesota: "I do not know as I am pre. pared to add very much to the arguments that have been presented in this paper by Dr. Grissom. I was educated in a hospital where mechanical restraint was used, and I still use it – always, I think, with discretion, as from time to time I have estimated the per centage, I have always found it less than two per cent., and with a number of patients exceeding five hundred."

Dr. STEVENS, Missouri: "I do not think of anything additional, bearing directly upon the question, but I wish it understood that I am decidedly in favor of mechanical restraint, as the matter seems to be understood by this body."

Dr. HUGHES, Missouri: "I am very much in accord with the tenor of Dr. Grissom's excellent paper. His title is well chosen. In some cases the problem of determining what kind of restraint should be employed is better solved by selecting protective mechanical, in preference to irritative physical restraint. I have had cases that I preferred to restrain by these safe, silent and passive appliances than to confine them to the tender mercies of over-taxed and irritable attendants."

Dr. BAUDNY, Missouri: "I deem it proper to occupy the time of this association but a few moments. So much has been said on the subject under discussion that there remains but very little to be added. In the year 1884, after having carefully perused Connolly's work, I became converted to his ideas, and caused every means of mechanical restraint in the asylum with which I am connected to be destroyed. A very short time elapsed, when several catastrophes occurred, which owed their origin to this cause. Not many more weeks passed, when I made a most narrow escape from serious injury by a blow inflicted on me by a maniac, which served as an *argumentum ad hominem* to make me reconsider my determination. One or two cases of suicide occurred. In every case no restraint was used. Since that time I have caused mechanical restraint to be applied in every case in which previous attempts at self-destruction had been made— that is to say, I have placed them in the muff until I was satisfied there was no further danger. Of two evils, it is better to choose the lesser; therefore, I consider it as neces- sary to use mechanical means of restraint as to employ medicinal measures. This applies to cases of melancholia as well as to those of masturbation, nymphomania, etc. My experience with this method of treatment has been such as to cause me to consider restraint as an indispensable means in the therapeutics of insanity—one which I should be unwilling to abandon.

"I may also say that, in conversation with patients who have recovered under treatment, I have never heard one complain of the use of mechanical restraint; on the other hand, they frequently complain of the attendants. None of them have ever asked that mechanical restraint be abolished from the asylum; on the contrary, there are certain patients who fear the coming on of attacks of violence, and ask to have restraint applied before the outbreak.

"Then, again, it seems to me that the use of mechanical restraint is much better than personal control, exercised by the hands of attendants. In cases of acute mania, it seems to me that the attempt to keep a patient quiet by the com- bined strength of three or four persons must be fraught with dangers. Indeed, I am satisfied that one death which I wit- nessed was caused by the attempt of a patient to free himself from the hands of the attendants who were trying to control him. I believe now that if the camisole had been placed upon him, instead of the hands of the nurses, he would be living to-day. The only forms of mechanical restraint ever in use in St. Vincent's Institution are the camisole, muff and anklet. One of the great advantages of the use of these appliances is, that patients can safely walk about the grounds, enjoy the fresh air and sunlight, and avoid the evils of close confinement.

"After long reflection on the entire subject, and having been once on the other side of the question, I must say that experience has taught me that we cannot dispense with mechanical restraint, and that the real question at issue is not as to their being absolutely essential, but that abuse of this method of treatment is to be guarded against."

Dr. HINDE, Missouri: "The time of the Association has been well occupied by members from Missouri, and yet, in the absence of our Superintendent, and seeing also that Dr. Catlett is absent from the hall, it is proper for me to state that the opinions and practice of our State Asylum at Fulton are entirely in accord with the able paper read by Dr. Grissom, and the views so forcibly expressed by Dr. Gray."

Dr. FULLER, Nebraska: "The limited experience which I have had in the care and treatment of the insane prohibits my taking any active part in the discussion of the subject in question. I wish, however, to give expression to the unqualified pleasure with which I listened to Dr. Grissom's article— a pleasure due not less to its rare literary merit than to the fact that the views expressed harmonized with my own."

Dr. BUCK, Ontario: "I have no desire to occupy the time of this meeting with any remarks of mine upon this subject, for I could add nothing to what has been already so fully and well said by Dr. Grissom in his able paper, and by those who have preceded me in the discussion of it."

Now let me call your attention to what some eminent authors, who are not connected with insane asylums, have to say on this subject.

I first read from "Spitka's Manual of Insanity":

"On the other hand, it must be admitted that the agitation against restraint has overstepped the bounds of legitimate criticism and reform. That there are some subjects who require restraint—who are better off with than without it—there can be no doubt. The demonstrative fact of a novice Superintendent who burned up all his restraining apparatus as soon as he took charge of his asylum, was followed by the accumulation of black eyes, broken noses, and other minor surgical accidents, as well as by several suicides. It should be remembered that Connolly, the very apostle of non-restraint, said: 'Without a very efficient superintendence, chiefly to be exercised by the chief medical officers, the mere absence of mechanical restraint may constitute no sufficient security against neglect, or even ill treatment of patients, in a large asylum. The medical officers who consider such watchful supervision not perfectly comprised in their duties have formed but a very inadequate conception of them.'"

Again, we find in "A System of Practical Medicine," by American authors, edited by William Pepper, M. D., LL. D., president and professor of the theory and practice of medicine and of chemical medicine in the University of Pennsylvania (edition of 1886), an article by Charles F. Folsom, M. D., in which the following occurs, viz.:

"Mechanical restraint increases the cerebral hyperæmia, and there are few homes or general hospitals where it must not be used, if there is excessive violence or delirium, making the insane asylum in those cases a necessity. Objectionable as it is, however, mechanical restraint is less harmful than the continued use of large doses of sedative drugs, as is often the practice in order to keep patients quiet enough to remain at home."

Again, in "Kirkbride on Hospitals for the Insane," by Thomas S. Kirkbride, M. D., LL.D., physician-in-chief and Superintendent of the Pennsylvania Hospital for the Insane, at Philadelphia, late President of the Association of Medical Superintendents of American Institutions for the Insane, honorary member of the British Medico-Psychological Association, etc., we find the following:

"And yet, without a proper force of attendants and sufficient classification, the use of mechanical means of restraint and the protracted seclusion of certain classes of patients, are almost unavoidable. Much has been said by writers, most generally by those not practically familiar with the treatment of the insane, in regard to a 'non-restraint' system of management and the treatment of all patients without restraint. This, it need hardly be suggested, is simply impossible. As soon as any person has lost the use of his reason, and has become irresponsible for his actions, just so soon is it manifestly necessary that he should be under the care of some one; and this care and control are, of themselves, restraint. What is commonly meant, is not that there is no restraining apparatus—no mechanical means of restraint are used. For most patients none of these are really required, but they are essential to the best interest of a very limited number of cases, and are more humane than having them controlled by the hands of attendants, whose perfect command of their own feelings and actions is not always to be trusted. The medical attendant of such a case, with a full knowledge of all its peculiarities, is the only proper judge of the propriety or impropriety of the application of these means of control, certainly a much better judge than any one who decides the question only from preconceived ideas and theoretical notions.

"Physicians may differ widely in regard to the particular forms of mechanical restraint that may be most desirable, but it is safe to say that they are few in number, simple in form and little repulsive in appearance. In my own experience, strong wristbands, soft leather mittens, connected linen sleeves, *and the apparatus for confining a patient in bed*, are all that are required; *the last named, in certain conditions of a patient, being of the utmost value, and often unquestionably a means of saving life.* My experience would indicate, that on an average not more than one or two per cent. of all the patients require any mechanical means of restraint; that often a period of several months may pass without their being needed, and that any superintendent may conduct an institution without applying them, in case he is anxious to avoid the criticism of pseudo-experts, and willing to let his patients lose the advantages that may result from their occasional use. At the same time, I am equally positive that a practical familiarity with this treatment will prevent any declarations like the positive dicta often heard in regard to this subject in many quarters. The number who now adopt these ultra views in reference to mechanical means of restraint in any case of insanity, is obviously diminishing, and it is to be hoped that before a long period the belief will be universal, that, while rarely necessary, yet, in some cases, they ought to be used, and that not to use them, when thus required, is neither professional nor does justice to the afflicted."

Thus it will be seen that Dr. Kirkbride shows and commends the great value *of the apparatus for confining a patient in bed*—the same apparatus that was so paraded and displayed before you by counsel on the other side as an instrument of torture and an evidence of barbarism. Verily, one would have thought from the display that was made of this common, useful and humane apparatus, that the counsel on the other side had found within these walls some relic of the Inquisition, and presented it to the horrified gaze of the members of this Board. In this connection, I wish to say that the asylum presided over by Dr. Kirkbride is a corporate institution, and that the most violent insane are not permitted to enter it; yet, he uses and approves of the kind of mechanical restraint practiced here. If these high and eminent authorities, and the fact that Dr. Grissom, after having openly and boldly advocated in print and by voice mechanical restraint, has been elevated to the highest honors in the gift of the Association of Superintendents and of the medical profession, satisfies you that mechanical restraint is not cruel *per se*, but, on the contrary, a proper and humane mode of treatment for the insane—as I think you must be satisfied—then it only remains to inquire whether Dr. Grissom has been guilty of abusing the use of mechanical restraint.

This brings us to the consideration of the specifications under the head of the second charge, which relates to cruelty to patients.

Before proceeding any further in the regular order of my remarks, permit me, gentlemen of the Board, to recur to the charge of immorality, and to the specification in which Dr. Grissom is charged with having been criminally intimate with Miss Nora Burch. For the purpose, I suppose, of contradicting Dr. Grissom's testimony, and that of Miss Burch's mother and sister, to the effect that Miss Burch suffered with *painful* menstruation, her commitment papers to the Morganton Asylum were offered in evidence by the other side. In these papers it is stated that *menstruation was regular*; and in this regard it will be claimed that the testimony of these witnesses and these papers are at variance. But there is no conflict—there is no variance. Fortunately, there are many skilled, able, and accomplished physicians on this Board; and there is not one of them who does not know that menstruation may be perfectly *regular as to periods,* and at the same time exceedingly *painful* on account of some abnormal position or condition of the uterus. The testimony is in harmony, and not in conflict.

And now again in regard to mechanical restraint:

I repeat, that under the two heads of immorality and cruelty, eight of the specifications are eliminated from your consideration, because not a scintilla of evidence was offered in support of them, and seven more should also be eliminated, because the sole and only witness to six of the seven is Ella N. Edwards and the only witness to the other is T. J. Harris— witnesses who have shown themselves to be totally unworthy of belief. Of the remaining specifications the following ought also to be eliminated from your consideration, because the only charge and evidence is that they were strapped to the bed, and not for any unusual length of time, and therefore, mechanical restraint, as I have abundantly shown you by eminent authority, not being *per se* cruel, no cruelty was practiced, viz.: Mike Cosgrove, Mr. Kennedy, Mr. Williams, Robert Barnett, Jonathan Bass, Zeb. Williams, Mr. Wortham and Mrs. Gaskins. The case of J. C. Hervey, the man who spit in Dr. Grissom's face and used most obscene, vulgar and loathsome language about his wife, ought also to be eliminated, because the only evidence against Dr. Grissom in this case is that he assisted the attendant in a violent struggle with this patient, and that in doing so he put his foot on his hip for the purpose of assisting in holding him down until he could be secured, and that Hervey was not in the slightest injured. The case of John Nutt ought also to be eliminated, because the only evidence against Dr. Grissom in his case is, that when he had called Dr. Grissom "a damned son of a bitch," and otherwise behaved in such a manner as to break up all discipline and set a bad example to other patients, Dr. Grissom merely pushed him back on the bed, not even inflicting a scratch on his person.

It is on such trivial matters as these that you are asked to brand with the stigma of disgrace this respondent. And now, what are the cases, under the head of cruelty, about which any evidence has been offered—any evidence that is seriously worthy of your consideration? They are as follows: W. P. Upchurch, Henry Cone, J. D. L. Smith and Mrs. Lowther.

And thus, Mr. President and gentlemen of the Board, all this fuss, and clamor, and parade about cruelty dwindles down to four cases, out of one thousand four hundred and ten patients treated during twenty-one years of service. After months, yes, years, of silent, stealthy, revengeful preparation on the part of the prosecutors, they come here with the pitiful showing of appearance—for I say it is only an appearance— of cruelty in four cases. Never before has this State been searched, from one end to the other, with such malignant industry for evidence, and never was result so insignificant. And now as to these four cases: The first is that of W. P. Upchurch, and it is the one upon which the prosecution mainly relies. The evidence in this case is that some *six years ago*, to-wit, *in the year* 1883, this patient, who is a desperate and danger- ous insane man—a man who has homicidal tendencies—a man who had, previous to his admission here, nearly shot to death an officer of the law, and had attempted to kill a mem- ber of his own family—a man who was sent here by the order of a criminal court—a man of desperate character, who, while in a towering rage, and endowed with demoniacal and superhuman strength, had wrenched from its fastening in his window an iron bar, and, armed with this deadly weapon, was raving, and cursing, and defying everybody and everything, and spreading terror and dismay through the wards. In this state of affairs, Dr. Grissom, Mr. Thomp- son (the Steward), who is one of the prosecutors here to-day, and two or three attendants, rushed in his room upon him, with a mattress, and threw him upon the floor. In the life- and-death struggle which ensued with this powerful maniac the witnesses do not agree as to what Dr. Grissom did and said. Mr. Thompson says that Dr. Grissom stamped Up- church in the face, and cursed him; Mr. Harris and Mr. Hogan say that he put his foot on his neck and cursed him; and Dr. Grissom says he merely put his foot on his body to help hold him down. The truth is that, in the great excite- ment of the moment, no one knows exactly what did take place. Mr. Thompson says that when he (Upchurch, got up his mouth was bleeding; but this was doubtless caused by his being violently thrown to the floor when the crowd rushed in upon him with the mattress. All the testimony shows there was no bruises upon him, and that he was not injured or hurt. And, furthermore, it is in evidence that Upchurch, while insane, had sense enough to know the object of restraint, and to know that he was doing wrong in defying all authority and spreading terror among the other patients, and thereby impeding their recovery. While Dr. Grissom, in the excitement natural to such a struggle with such a powerful and dangerous man, might have used some excessive force in this case, he did nothing more than what frail human nature is liable to do under such circumstances. Superintendents are human and frail, like the rest of us, and liable, when greatly excited, to make mistakes. Many of us have heard of physicians who, when angered, have perhaps slapped a child for biting them, etc., or of policemen who sometimes, without intending it, have used excessive force, yet no one thought of trying to bring disgrace upon them for so doing. Neither does the statute under which we are proceeding require that a superintendent shall have the patience of Job or the meekness of John, or that he shall be removed for cruelty, where no intent to be cruel is shown. There is not a man on that Board but knows that Dr. Grissom was never intentionally cruel to anybody or anything.

But there is another matter connected with this Upchurch case, and the prosecutors in this matter, that must strike every man of common sense as strange and wonderful. It is this: Mr. Thompson and Dr. Rogers prepared a report of this very Upchurch case, to be read by Dr. Grissom before the " Association of American Superintendents of Insane Asylums," and it was read by him. When this report was prepared Dr. Rogers had not begun to plot and conspire against his benefactor, and Mr. Thompson had not had a fight with Dr. Grissom's son. The report is as follows:

"W. P. Upchurch : Admitted June 12th, 1878; male; single; farmer; is homicidal, shot his brother and has attempted to kill other people. He has terrible delusions, connected with others, that his bones, his head, neck, etc., are crushed; has hallucinations of hearing—hears people talking about him, planning to kill him, etc. *On one occasion he kicked an iron bar out of his window-guard, and defied any one to come to him.* Is a large, powerful man and exceedingly dangerous. Often wakes up and tears up his bed-clothes, clothing and everything within his reach. His attacks upon people are sudden and without warning, and, except for restraint, would occur at least two or three times per day."

Remember, this report was gotten up by Dr. Rogers and Mr. Thompson, as an evidence of the beneficial results of mechanical restraint, and was so used by Dr. Grissom. Do you find anything in it about cruelty? Can it be possible that so high-toned and honorable men as the prosecutors are—men who are only actuated by motives of the public good in this prosecution—could make such a report of the Upchurch case as to commend his treatment to all the superintendents of insane asylums in the United States, when all the time they knew that the treatment of Upchurch had been attended with the cruelty and barbarity they would now have you believe it was? Could such men be parties to such a fraud? They would have you to believe that as public guardians of good morals, and as avengers of Upchurch's wrongs, they now stand on the watch-tower to proclaim to the world the wrong-doing of this respondent. I ask, if they are such now, what were they when they made that report—when they loaned themselves to such a fraud and imposition on the people of North Carolina? Were they the courageous defenders of the unfortunate insane then, or is it only lately they have assumed that part? They are at liberty to take either horn of the dilemma, and make the most of it.

The next case is that of Henry Cone, and the evidence in regard to him is that he is a powerful man and a desperate

character, and that he had the habit of springing una-
wares—like a Bengal tiger from his lair—on any one who
was near; that on one occasion, when in one of his maniacal
fits, with countenance suffused with rage and blood, he
jumped, like a tiger on his prey, upon the Superintendent,
who, for self-protection, and for the purpose of diminishing
the flow of blood to the head and quieting him, put his
hands on each side of his neck and pressed the carotid arte-
ries, choking him about one minute, and afterwards threw
water in his face; that in ten or twelve minutes afterwards
he was sitting on the bench in the hall, and had no bruises
on him, and required no medical attention. He was not in
the least hurt, and the treatment he received has greatly
improved him, and he has now ceased to jump on people.

The next case is that of J. D. L. Smith, a very dangerous
criminal, sent to the asylum by order of a criminal court—so
dangerous that there was a standing order in the institution
that, on no account, was an attendant ever to go into his
room alone—so dangerous that he had to be fed through a
trap-door—a man who conceals matches in his bed for the
purpose of setting the institution on fire—(he was sent to the
asylum for burning a bridge across the Cape Fear River)—
a man who tried, time and again, to commit suicide by
biting his arm and cutting himself with pieces of tin, etc.—
the most mischievous patient who has ever been within the
walls of the asylum—engaged all the time in making false
keys, and with them unlocking doors and windows, and
who has escaped twice. As to him, it is charged that Dr.
Grissom, on one occasion, when greatly provoked, lost his
temper and indulged in some profanity; and the testimony
is, that he frequently had Smith strapped to the bed, for the
purpose of preventing him from injuring himself or some
other patient, and for the purpose of impressing him with
the impropriety of his conduct. It is also in evidence that
during these periods of strapping to the bed, he was frequently released in order that he might get his meals, attend

to the calls of nature, and for the purpose of resting him; that he has sense enough to know the object for which he is strapped, and to know the difference between right and wrong, and that the treatment he has received has greatly improved him, and he now goes about with the other patients; whereas, formerly he had to be confined in the "strong-room" most of the time. The next, and last case, is that of Mrs. Lowther; and the evidence in regard to her is, that she was a very violent patient—frequently fighting other patients, and defying all rules of discipline in the institution, and that for the purpose of controlling her and impressing her with the impropriety of her conduct, she was strapped on two succeeding days, but was frequently released, in the meanwhile, for the purpose of getting her meals, attending to the calls of nature, and of being rested; that on the second day after she was released finally, she got up ate a meal, took a bath, and in about two hours afterwards died, from what was supposed to be heart disease. Had her death not occurred at the time it did, we never would have heard of this case in this trial, for no one would have alleged cruelty in her case. It will be argued to you, on the other side, that her death was caused by the strapping to the bed, yet I defy any one to show any evidence that such was the case. It was just one of those sudden deaths that might have happened at any time, and do happen every day. There is not a physician on that Board who is not familiar with such cases. Why, I remember, not long ago, to have seen an article published by one of the most eminent physicians in the South, and an honored citizen of an adjoining State, in which he gave an account of how two of his patients died while under the influence of chloroform, administered by himself, and yet no one thought of charging him with cruelty, or preferring charges against him intended to humiliate and degrade him. Mrs. Lowther's death was just one of those sudden, unfortunate deaths, that might have, and I suppose has occurred, in the experience of every physician of any practice in this State or any other State. Mrs. Lowther died some *five years ago*, and at that time the prosecutors did not think strapping to the bed for two days was cruel, because at the same time they got up a report of the Upchurch case for Dr. Grissom to read at the meeting of the Superintendents; they also got up reports of the cases of Mrs. Mary M. Morse and Mrs. M. S. Brown, which are as follows, viz.:

"M. S. BROWN: Admitted May 17, 1882; forty-four years old; female; married; well educated; housewife; Methodist; in health, gentle, retiring disposition—amiable and pleasant. Puerperal 'insanity; child born on March 9; insanity manifested on March 13 by despondency, attempts to kill her child and determined attempts to kill herself; also made attempts to kill her husband. Her suicidal tendency became very violent. Her whole aim and purpose seemed to be to kill herself in any possible way—by choking herself, dashing herself against the floor or wall, or any way she could. It was impossible to prevent her injuring herself some, without restraining her. Her movements were so quick and sudden that she would dash herself to the floor before any one could detain her, even though sitting beside her. She was restrained to the bed, *night and day, except when taken up for necessary purposes and for rest, and remained so most of the time.* She has been so until some two months ago; since then she has been released, most of the time, though an attendant sits with her constantly, and seldom permits her to go beyond her reach."

"MARY M. MORSE: Admitted December 2, 1883; twenty-six years old; female; married; no children; housewife; Baptist; common education. In health, well disposed and cheerful; good habits; always was "nervous;" mother was insane with a tendency to suicide. This is her third attack. At the time of her second attack she was treated at the insane asylum at Columbia, S. C.; was discharged after some months, much improved; remained improved three or four months, then had a relapse; makes violent and determined attempts at suicide. On admission she was deeply depressed; knows where she is and why brought here; answers questions intelligently, and when she can be aroused talks pretty well. Her first night, on entering the dining-room at supper time, she seized a knife and attempted to kill herself. Her suicidal tendency became so violent that she could not be left alone a moment, and, even with an attendant at her side, she would dash herself against the wall or floor, choke herself, etc. Nothing has any effect in breaking her determination. After a few days she was strapped to the bed, and even there she would try to bite herself, to strike herself against the bed, etc. *She was in restraint twelve days, except when up for rest, etc.* Her determination seemed to weaken, and on the twelfth day, after promising, voluntarily, that she would not attempt it again, she was released. For five days she kept her promise, but on the fifth day her resolution gave way, and she became as violently suicidal as ever, and was again restrained. *After eight days she again became better, and begged to be released,* promising never to attempt suicide again. She was released, and has constantly improved, and never has made another attempt at suicide. She is now in the convalescent ward. Since her release and improvement her husband died, but she showed no unnatural grief, and bore the trial with fortitude and submissive resignation."

Now, it is evident that the prosecutors did not think, at that time, *that restraining for more than twelve days at a time was cruel,* else they would not have lent themselves to making a report for Dr. Grissom to read to the Association for the purpose of sustaining his article on the humanity and beneficial results of mechanical restraint. It is also evident that the " Association of American Superintendents of Insane Asylums " did not so regard it, else they would not have commended his article, as it was commended, or have afterwards honored him with every place of honor and trust in their gift, as they did. It is also inconceivable that gentlemen of such lofty character as the prosecutors are—gentlemen who are actuated alone by high and noble motives of public good—should, if they thought, as they say they do, that Mrs. Lowther was murdered through Dr. Grissom's cruelty, *keep silent about it for five long years;* should remain in the employment of, and associated with, a murderer of a poor insane woman for five long years and never breathe a word of it to a member of the Board, or to a legislative committee, or a magistrate, or to any relative or friend of the murdered woman, or to any living soul. Mr. President, and gentlemen of the Board, what language can characterize such championship of the afflicted and the oppressed? How can such motives of public good be sufficiently commended? A few more words on this subject of restraint, and I leave it. It is evident that when Dr. Grissom had mechanical restraint applied to patients many of these attendants, not understanding his motive, or the purpose for which it was used, thought him cruel; so they would probably think a physician who would wrap a patient in a plaster jacket, or fit a leg in an apparatus that prevents any turning or bending of the limb, for the purpose of curing some deformity. Yet you, gentlemen, especially those of you who are physicians, know better; you also know that it is absolutely necessary to maintain some kind of order and discipline in the institution if you would avoid a perfect pandemonium; and this in order that the violent and incurable may not be permitted to so conduct themselves as to render worse the condition of the harmless and curable. To do this, some kind of restraint is necessary, either manual or mechanical. The former cannot be adopted here, because the appropriation for the support of the institution is not sufficient to enable the Superintendent to employ four or five attendants for every violent insane patient. That may do for some of the rich private asylums of the North, but not for this one. But leaving this out of consideration, I think I have shown you that mechanical restraint is preferable anyhow. When to use mechanical restraint, and how to use it, must, of necessity, be left to the discretion of the Superintendent. He is a far better judge than are discharged employees, or than you can be, without seeing the patient or being acquainted with all the surrounding circumstances. The remarkably low death-rate, and the large percentage of recoveries here, show that it has not been abused by the Superintendent. For, remember, that there has been only one homicide, and not a single suicide, during the twenty-one years of this Superintendent's administration.

As to the third charge, that of misappropriation, I do not think it amounts to enough to detain you with a discussion of it. The counsel on the other side evidently think so, too, and have said as much in open court. We have shown you an order of the Board allowing Dr. Grissom to have anything from or raised on the premises, and that ends the question, because the turkeys and the celery, etc., were raised and grown on the Asylum premises. As to the $500, he admits that, in pursuance of an order of the Board, he has been buying provisions from the Steward, and that there is now a balance of $500 due by him, which he is ready, willing and able to pay. This indebtedness has all along been known to the Board, and there has never been any attempt at concealment of this or any other matter under this head. There has never been any evil intent, any element of a crime, about anything testified to under this third charge ; and the most that could be made out of *the pie and chicken business* would be to charge Dr. Grissom's account with half a dozen spring chickens and two or three pies. Hence, I say I will not detain you on this charge.

It is hard to believe that Mr. Thompson and Dr. Rogers are actuated by motives of the public good in this prosecution, for had they been, when they were bringing witnesses to testify as to the turkeys of Mrs. Lawrence feeding on asylum scraps, why did they not tell about those of Mr. West, the engineer? Were they silent because Mr. West sided with them in this prosecution? When they were telling about the company Mrs. Lawrence, the Matron, sometimes entertained here, why did they not tell about the company Dr. Rogers entertained at the expense of the institution? And why, O why, if their motives are good and righteous, did they not sooner report some of the villany they now complain of to some member of the Board or committee of the Legislature? Their conduct in this regard is incomprehensible. Another thing that is peculiar in this case is that, *of the one thousand four hundred and ten patients* treated here by Dr. Grissom, not *one* can the prosecutors get to come here and testify as to his misconduct in any regard; on the contrary, they uniformly testify in his behalf. And again, of all the female attendants who are here now or have ever been here, with the solitary exception of "wild-cat" Ella N. Edwards, not one can be found to come here and testify as to the immorality or cruelty of this man; on the contrary, they, with one accord, testify as to his good behavior and gentlemanly conduct. Who, then, is it that does testify against him? It is mainly discharged male employees, into whose ears the poison of these prosecutors has been distilled. That letter of Dr. Rogers' discloses as dark and deep and damnable a plot as was ever hatched in hell; it shows the machinations of the seducer of women and the suborner of witnesses; and its poison has infused itself into the whole current of the prosecutors' testimony, and tainted and contaminated it all, and rendered it unworthy of credit or belief; it shows that one of the prosecutors has been engaged in manufacturing testimony, and that fact once proven or admitted, every particle of evidence offered by the prosecution is discredited and not to be relied upon. From the beginning of this trial you have been threatened by the prosecutors with what the public would do if you dared to decide against them. Such threats will have no terrors for you, but you will decide this case according to the evidence, and without fear and without favor.

Mr. President, and gentlemen of the Board, a few more words, and I have done. You have in your hands the making or the unmaking of one of North Carolina's brightest and most honored sons. Born to poverty and humble birth, with no fortune but his talents, and no friend but his industry, he rushed into the ranks where wealth and talent and influence had arrayed themselves, and he became the peer of the foremost. No man in this State has had more blushing honors conferred upon him, or worn them more gracefully, than has the distinguished accused. Abandoning twenty years ago the bright prospects and allurements of public life and the pleasures and comforts of home, he has lived and reared his family amid the terrors and horrors of an insane asylum, and devoted the best years of his life to the alleviation of the sufferings of the unfortunate and afflicted

The evidence adduced in this trial before you shows what that life has been. It shows you, among other things, that he has been spit upon, cursed, struck, choked, the receiver of vulgar notes, and the object of indecent language in regard to himself and his wife; that his kindness to the prosecutors has been repaid by insubordination and ingratitude; that he has been surrounded by secret enemies and spies, who have been sedulously sowing the seeds of treachery and discord, and seeking by every means, fair and foul, to compass his ruin.

As a consequence and culmination of all this, he stands before you to-day on trial. He does not *beg* for mercy, but he *demands*, in the name of justice and fair play, that, on the tainted and manufactured evidence offered you in this trial by the prosecutors, you do not rob him, his wife and his children, of that which is more precious to him and them than his life—his good name and his great reputation, honorably earned by many years of service in the cause of afflicted and sorrowing humanity.

Mr. President, and gentlemen of the Board, I thank you for the patient hearing which you have accorded me.

www.ingramcontent.com/pod-product-compliance
Lightning Source LLC
Chambersburg PA
CBHW031822090426
42739CB00008B/1377